We Remember, We Build
An Anthology of Truth, Resistance, and Reclamation

By T.E. Door

We Remember, We Build

Copyright © 2025 by Tanesha Door

All rights reserved. No part of this publication may be reproduced, stored in a retrieval system, or transmitted in any form or by any means—electronic, mechanical, photocopying, recording, or otherwise—without the prior written permission of the author, except for brief quotations used in reviews, academic critique, or by journalists in accordance with fair use laws.

This anthology is an original work composed of essays, poetry, and creative nonfiction grounded in personal truth, historical analysis, and communal memory. Unless otherwise noted, all writing is original and written by T.E. Door.

Select essays and poems draw inspiration from real events, sourced historical records, and national headlines. All citations are included in the References & Acknowledgments section. Names or details may have been changed to protect privacy.

Cover art and interior design by T.E. Door

Edited and developed by T.E. Door and collaborative creative advisors

First Edition

Published in Atlanta, Georgia, USA

Printed in the United States of America

ISBN: 979-8-218-66167-0

Library of Congress Control Number: 2025908941

Publisher: Tawitit Village Publishers

For permissions or inquiries, contact: tawititvillagepublishers@blakmindentertainment.com

Table of Contents

Benediction……………………………………………………………………………….5

Prologue: The Machine We Were Born Into……………………………………...6

The System We Serve, The Future We Deserve…………………………………………...6

Poem: Chains in Disguise, Power Reclaimed…………………………………………...9

PART ONE: THE SYSTEM OF CONTROL
Exposing how modern power structures mirror slavery and systemic oppression…………………………...11

The Plantation Never Burned: How Governments Hold Power Like Slaveholders…………………………………………………………………………..12
Poem: The Plantation Never Burned……………………………………………..16

The Overseers Still Ride: How Law Enforcement Maintains Control……………...21
Poem: "Hands Up, Don't…"……………………………………………………...24
Masters of the Modern Age: How Political Sponsors Own the System……………...32
Poem: Strings Attached…………………………………………………………..38
Labor in Chains: How Workers and Children Remain Enslaved to Capitalism……………...43
Poem: First Bell…………………………………………………………………..47

PART TWO: THE BREAKING POINT
How resistance rises and the system fights back……………………………………...50

The War on Truth: How Media and Misinformation Keep the Chains Tight………..51
Poem: Every Headline a Chain, Every Silence a Lock…………………………….57
Silencing the Fire: How the System Crushes Revolution…………………………….58
Poem: "The Pulpit Ain't the People"……………………………………………...63
The Myth of Reform: Why Change Can't Come from the System That Enslaved Us………66
Poem: "What's Gonna Change?"…………………………………………………...71
The Boiling Point: When the People Refuse to Bend……………………………….74
Poem: In the Middle of the Fireline………………………………………………...78

PART THREE: RECLAIMING POWER
How we take back what was stolen and build a new system on our own terms…………………………...81

From the Fields to the Throne: Black Leaders and Self-Governance……………………..…82
Poem: "I Don't Wear the Crown, But I Carry the Weight" ……………………………....86
Water from the People: Economic Freedom and Wealth Distribution……………….…..88
Poem: "The Vault Didn't Save Me" ……………………………………………………....92
Building Beyond the System: Reclaiming Land, Education, and Community…………….....96
Poem: "I Am the Land, and I Remember" ……………………………………..…..101

Epilogue
Poem: We Remember, We Build……………………………………………...…..104

Final Gesture……………………………………………………………...………...107

References & Acknowledgments…………………………………….…..………….108

Personal and Collective Gratitude……………………………………..…………..110

About the Author: T.E. Door………………………………………...……………..111

Benediction

May your voice rise like sunlight.

May your hands build what was never given.

And may you remember—

you are already enough to change everything..

Prologue: The Machine We Were Born Into

The System We Serve, The Future We Deserve

You've been told that slavery ended. That the past is the past. That the chains were broken, the fields abandoned, and that today's society is free.

But look again.

The chains didn't disappear. They were redesigned. The plantation was not burned—it was paved over, renamed, and expanded. What once bound the body now binds the mind, the wallet, the law. The system that fed on Black bodies for centuries is still here, still feeding, still grinding us down—just under new names.

And you, reader, are in it. You are either breaking chains, or reinforcing them.

The Slaveholders Didn't Leave—They Took Office

Do you think slavery ended because the laws changed? Because a document declared it so? No. Slavery evolved, and its masters became governors and mayors, sitting in high-rise offices instead of plantations. They no longer need whips to control you when they can do it with policies, zoning laws, and wages that keep you locked in the fields—now called factories, office buildings, underfunded schools, and prisons.

Do you wonder why the minimum wage never keeps up with inflation? Why affordable housing is pushed further out of reach? Why public schools in Black neighborhoods crumble while police budgets grow?

That's not a failure of the system. That is the system. The same hands that once signed slave codes now sign bills to suppress votes, defund education, and cut social services—all while ensuring the wealthy keep getting richer.

The plantation never disappeared. It became the city. And its overseers became your elected officials.

The Slave Handlers Don't Carry Whips—They Carry Badges

And what about the enforcers? The men who once rode horseback, hunting down those who ran, those who resisted? They still exist. They just have new titles—FBI. CIA. Local police. Homeland Security.

They don't call it slave patrol anymore. They call it law enforcement. But what do they really enforce?

They enforced Jim Crow.

They enforced COINTELPRO, spying on and dismantling Black leaders like Malcolm X, MLK, and Fred Hampton.

They enforced the War on Drugs, flooding Black communities with crack cocaine, then locking up generations of our people in cages.

They enforce surveillance today, watching every movement, tapping every phone, waiting to silence those who resist.

They don't need whips when they have cameras, prison bars, and bullets. They don't need auctions when they have for-profit prisons and police quotas.

And yet, the narrative remains: trust the system, follow the rules, obey. But tell me—when has obedience ever led us to freedom?

The Masters No Longer Walk the Fields—They Fund the Machine

Who controls it all? Who pulls the strings? Who profits while we labor?

The names are different, but the role remains the same. Once, they were the slave masters—wealthy men in grand estates who controlled the economy. Today, they are called corporate donors, political sponsors, and billionaires.

They don't need to own you physically when they can own the laws that govern you.

They pay for campaigns. They choose your leaders before you ever get a vote.

They fund wars for profit, while telling you there's no money for healthcare or education.

They ensure wages remain low, while their wealth multiplies.

They decide who eats and who starves, who lives comfortably and who struggles just to breathe.

They never needed to crack a whip themselves. They have always paid others to do it for them.

The Slaves of Today Punch a Clock Instead of Picking Cotton

And now, look around. Who keeps this system running? Who fills the fields, the factories, the prisons?

Workers. Children. You.

The field is no longer a plantation—it is a 9-to-5 that pays just enough to keep you alive, but never enough to let you leave.

The chains are no longer iron—they are debt, bills, and wages that never rise.

The overseers are no longer white men with whips—they are corporations, landlords, and politicians who tell you to "work harder" while stealing the wealth of your labor.

And what about the children? Born into debt, raised in underfunded schools, funneled into a system designed to either exploit them or imprison them.

This is not freedom. This is not progress. This is slavery with a new face.

But the Chains Are Breaking—Because We Are Breaking Them

But here's the truth they don't want you to see: the system is cracking.

For the first time, the hands that once tilled the soil now hold the pens that write the laws.

For the first time, the voices once drowned out now command the airwaves, the courtrooms, the boardrooms.

For the first time, the watched and the policed now sit in the very agencies that once hunted them.

For the first time, the children who were set up to fail are breaking the cycle, building something new.

This is what they fear most. Not rebellion. Not protest. Power. Real, unfiltered, unbought power.

So, what side of history will you stand on?

Will you be the one who keeps the machine running? Or will you be the one who tears it apart?

The chains have not disappeared. But they are being broken.

And those who once wore them are now the ones holding the keys.

Chains in Disguise, Power Reclaimed

The slaveholders sit in high-rise halls,

now called mayors and governors,

inking policies with the same old hands,

redrawing borders, renaming chains.

They speak of order, of growth, of law,

while the fields of labor stretch beneath them,

plowed by those who will never taste the harvest.

The slave handlers move in shadows,

now called the CIA and FBI,

watching, listening, silencing.

Not with whips, but with files,

not with shackles, but surveillance,

controlling the restless, punishing the bold,

ensuring that no worker forgets their place.

The masters never step onto the field,

never feel the weight of the sun

They sit behind curtains,

now called political sponsors,

writing checks that buy obedience,

funding the machine, fueling the lie.

Their wealth is the law, their influence the whip.

They do not command—they own.

And the slaves—they wake before the dawn.

They punch the clock,

raise the children,

build the towers,

pave the roads,

serve the food,

clean the dirt,

fight the wars.

They say the old world is gone,

but the system remains.

The names have changed,

but the labor is the same.

But today—

Some of those hands that once tilled the soil

now hold the pens that sign the laws.

Some of those voices once drowned in silence

now hold the mics, now command the rooms.

The chains do not disappear—

they must be broken.

And this time—

we are the ones breaking them.

PART ONE

THE SYSTEM OF CONTROL

exposing how modern power structures mirror slavery and systemic oppression

The Plantation Never Burned

How Governments Hold Power Like Slaveholders

Governments like to tell us that history moves forward, that we are far removed from the days when human beings were bought and sold, when entire communities were built on the backs of free labor. But power doesn't dissolve—it adapts. The same forces that once upheld the plantation economy still exist today, ensuring that those who were never meant to have power remain at the bottom.

Slavery wasn't just about owning bodies. It was about owning wealth, owning labor, and owning the future itself. When outright ownership became illegal, the system found new ways to control. Now, the plantation stretches across cities, courts, workplaces, and financial institutions, ensuring that while names have changed, the structure of control remains intact.

We were never freed. The plantation just expanded.

The Lawmakers Who Inherited the Master's House

When the Civil War ended, the men who once owned people as property didn't simply disappear. Many of them went into politics, became judges, controlled state economies, and rewrote laws to ensure their dominance remained untouched. They no longer needed chains when they had legislatures. They no longer needed slave patrols when they could build police forces. They no longer needed to physically brand a person when they could mark them with a criminal record.

Reconstruction was supposed to be a time of rebuilding, but for those who had spent centuries profiting from free labor, it was a period of restructuring control.

The plantation owners of the past evolved into the politicians and policymakers of today, still dictating:

- Who has access to land and housing.
- Which communities receive resources.
- Who gets to build wealth and who is denied.
- Who faces punishment, who is protected, and who is invisible to the system altogether.

They no longer call it slavery, but they keep people trapped in cycles that make freedom impossible. They tell people to "pull themselves up by their bootstraps" while ensuring that boots never make it onto their feet.

Governors and lawmakers control more than policies—they control survival itself.

A Rigged Economy That Keeps Power at the Top

The promise of hard work leading to success is a myth designed to keep people compliant. Those in power understand that if wealth was truly available to everyone, there would be no permanent underclass to exploit.

The financial system operates much like the plantation economy—only instead of chains, it uses debt, inflation, and stagnant wages to keep workers stuck in place.

- Wealth was built on stolen labor, yet those who generated it were denied access to it.
- Black communities were redlined out of generational wealth, kept in neighborhoods where resources were deliberately withheld.
- Public schools in low-income areas were designed not to create leaders, but to create workers who would accept survival as their only option.

Today, wages remain low while the cost of living skyrockets. Workers are expected to be grateful for jobs that barely pay rent, while corporations report record profits. Economic freedom is dangled in front of people like a prize they'll never reach—always close enough to see, never close enough to grasp.

And when the economy no longer has use for someone? There is another system waiting to absorb them.

The Criminal Justice System: A New Economy for the Same Old Labor

Slavery was never fully abolished—it was rewritten. The 13th Amendment states that slavery is illegal, except as punishment for a crime. That exception became the foundation for mass incarceration, turning prisons into modern-day plantations where labor is extracted for free.

- Black men were arrested in droves under "vagrancy" laws, forcing them into convict leasing—essentially re-enslaving them.
- The prison population exploded as industries realized they could profit from inmate labor without having to pay fair wages.
- Private prison companies struck deals with states to keep cells full, ensuring that a steady flow of people would be funneled into the system.

Prison labor now fuels industries across the country. Inmates manufacture furniture, sew clothing, and even fight fires—all while earning cents on the dollar, or nothing at all. They are forced to work, and if they refuse, they face punishment, solitary confinement, or loss of privileges.

The plantation model was simple: extract labor for profit and dispose of those who could no longer produce.

The prison system operates the same way.

Land Theft and Displacement: A Legacy That Never Ended

For centuries, Black people in America have been stripped of land, homes, and financial security. The methods have changed, but the result is always the same: displacement, instability, and the destruction of generational wealth.

- After the Civil War, Black farmers were promised land through the Freedmen's Bureau, only to have it taken away by legal loopholes and white violence.
- In the 20th century, redlining made it nearly impossible for Black families to buy homes in high-value neighborhoods.
- Urban renewal projects bulldozed Black communities under the guise of "progress," while white suburbs flourished.

And today, gentrification continues the same cycle.

Developers buy up land in historically Black neighborhoods, raising property taxes and rent until the original residents can no longer afford to stay. Landlords force out tenants with eviction tactics that aren't illegal, but should be. Homeowners are pressured into selling for far less than their property is worth, only for that land to be flipped for millions.

Wealth is not lost—it is transferred. The same system that denied people property now forces them out of the little they have left.

Governments do not intervene. Because displacement was always part of the design.

The Overseers Still Patrol, Just Under a Different Name

Slave patrols were designed to track down runaways, prevent rebellion, and punish those who resisted. They eventually became what we now call law enforcement.

- During Reconstruction, police enforced Black Codes and arrested freed slaves for "crimes" like unemployment.
- During the Civil Rights Movement, law enforcement brutally attacked those who demanded equality.
- Today, Black communities are over-policed, criminalized, and incarcerated at higher rates than any other group.

Policing was never about public safety. It was about maintaining social order, keeping those in power safe, and keeping those at the bottom in check.

The more things change, the more they stay the same.

This System Was Designed to Last—Unless We Destroy It

The structures that uphold oppression were not built overnight, and they will not crumble easily. Every piece of this system—from the economy to the justice system to housing policies—works together to maintain the same hierarchy that existed centuries ago.

They tell us the past is behind us, but we are still living in its shadow.

They tell us to follow the rules, but those rules were written to keep us in place.

They tell us to be patient, but we have waited long enough.

This system will not reform itself. It will not loosen its grip willingly. It must be forced to release what it has stolen.

The plantation never burned.

But it will.

The Plantation Never Burned

They rewrote the ledgers, but the debt never cleared.

Rebranded the fields, but the labor never changed.

Painted over the past, but the blood still seeps through.

The system didn't collapse—it was restructured.

The chains didn't shatter—they were refitted.

And the plantation? It never burned.

They don't call them slaveholders anymore.

Now, they call them mayors and governors—

but the role is the same.

Still dictating who eats and who starves,

who belongs and who is displaced,

who walks free and who is buried under a system

that calls oppression justice,

that calls control democracy,

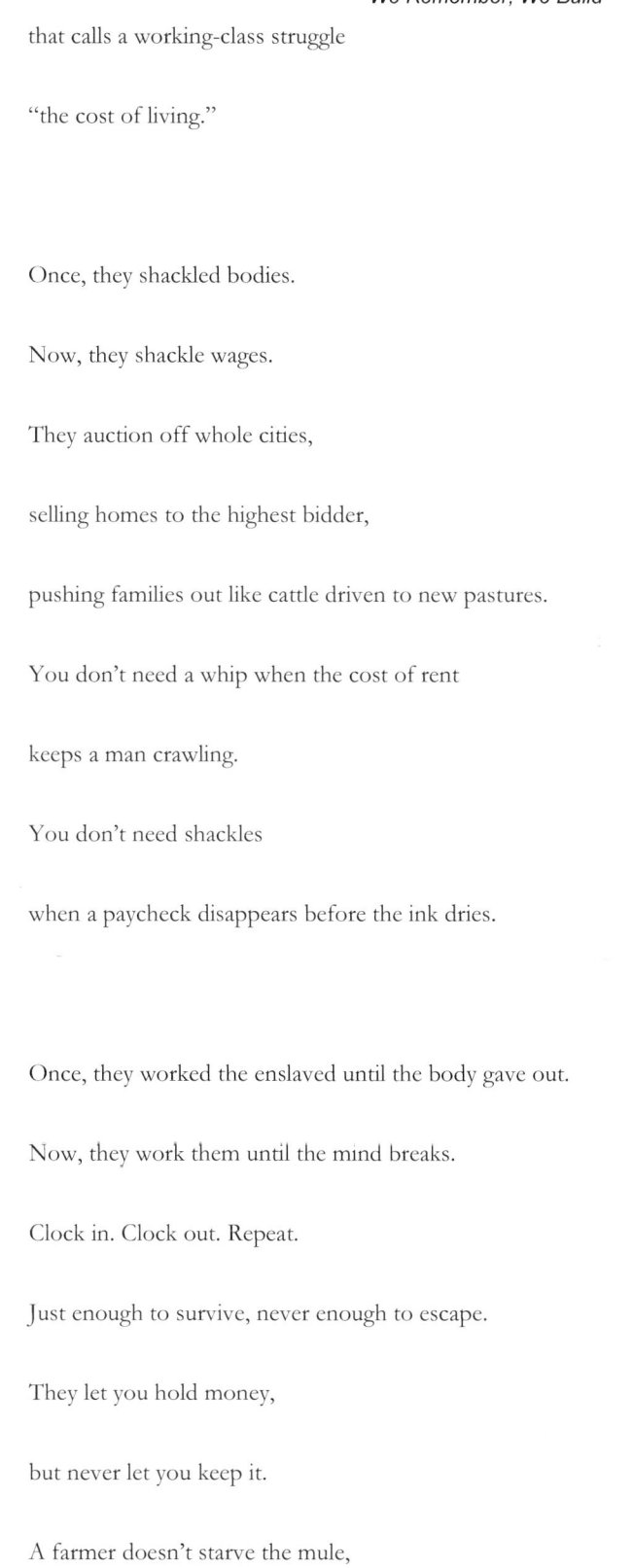

that calls a working-class struggle

"the cost of living."

Once, they shackled bodies.

Now, they shackle wages.

They auction off whole cities,

selling homes to the highest bidder,

pushing families out like cattle driven to new pastures.

You don't need a whip when the cost of rent

keeps a man crawling.

You don't need shackles

when a paycheck disappears before the ink dries.

Once, they worked the enslaved until the body gave out.

Now, they work them until the mind breaks.

Clock in. Clock out. Repeat.

Just enough to survive, never enough to escape.

They let you hold money,

but never let you keep it.

A farmer doesn't starve the mule,

but he never feeds it enough to run.

They never outlawed slavery.

They just gave it a clause,

stitched a loophole into the Constitution,

buried the chains inside the justice system.

Except as punishment for a crime—

and suddenly, Black men filled the prisons.

Convict leasing replaced the plantation,

chain gangs paved the roads,

and prison industries lined the pockets

of men whose grandfathers

bought bodies the old-fashioned way.

And when the fields became factories,

when the machines replaced hands,

they found new crops to harvest:

Debt. Labor. Incarceration.

They tell you work is the road to freedom,

but the road is a treadmill.

Run all you want,

you're still in the same place.

Still property.

Still controlled.

Still valuable only as long as your labor is useful.

And when it's not?

They still have the overseers.

Still armed. Still watching.

Still trained to put you down if you step out of line.

They don't call them slave catchers anymore,

but they serve the same purpose.

Badge, patrol, prison.

Lock, chain, sentence.

One slip, and you're back in the system,

filling the quotas, serving the machine.

They still need hands to build,

bodies to burn,

workers to break,

a whole class of people stuck in place,

digging the trenches of an empire

they will never be allowed to own.

The plantation never burned.

It just got better at hiding.

But fire spreads quick in dry fields.

And we are done waiting for permission to rise.

The match is already lit.

The Overseers Still Ride

How Law Enforcement Maintains Control

Policing in America is not about safety. It is about preserving an order that benefits the powerful at the expense of the powerless. It does not exist to prevent crime—it exists to manage the people that the system does not want to see rise.

Every empire needs enforcers. Every ruling class needs guards. The police are not public servants. They are the muscle of the political elite.

They are not here to solve problems. They are here to contain them.

When the people step outside the boundaries of what is acceptable, when the poor demand dignity, when the exploited push back, police forces mobilize—not as protectors, but as the front lines of suppression.

They are the system's enforcers, and their job is simple: Keep the people in their place.

A Manufactured Threat: How Police Create the Problems They Claim to Solve

There is a lie at the center of American policing: that without them, society would fall apart. That law enforcement is the only thing standing between order and chaos.

But look closely.

Where does the chaos come from? Who benefits from the disorder?

- Police over-police poor communities while ignoring crime in wealthy areas.
- They use minor offenses—loitering, jaywalking, petty theft—as a gateway to arrest and incarceration.
- They escalate situations instead of de-escalating, turning routine stops into violent encounters.
- They arrest people in bulk, ensuring that crime statistics always justify their presence.

And then they point to the chaos they create and call themselves the solution.

They fund themselves off of traffic stops and court fees that trap people in cycles of debt.

They seize money and property through civil asset forfeiture without ever proving a crime was committed.

They make arrests to fill quotas, knowing that a "tough on crime" stance means bigger budgets, more weapons, and more authority.

Police do not fight crime. They manufacture it.

Who Do the Police Serve? Follow the Money.

If police exist to keep us safe, why do they always protect property over people?

- Workers strike for better pay? Police show up to protect the company, not the workers.
- Tenants protest slumlords? Police evict them, instead of holding landlords accountable.
- Corporations pollute drinking water? Police arrest protesters, not the executives poisoning communities.

When billionaires feel threatened, police line up in riot gear.

When poor people feel threatened, police are nowhere to be found.

They do not stop crime, because crime is not the enemy of the system. Poverty is. Disobedience is. Resistance is.

And when the people rise up, police make it clear: their allegiance is to power.

Suppressing Revolt: When the System is Threatened, the Police Show Their True Purpose

The fastest way to understand the role of law enforcement is to watch what happens when people challenge the system.

- The Civil Rights Movement? Met with fire hoses, attack dogs, and mass arrests.
- The Black Panther Party? Infiltrated, framed, and assassinated by the FBI.
- The George Floyd protests? Tear gas, rubber bullets, and thousands of beatings in the streets.

Time and time again, when the people demand justice, police are the first to answer—not with solutions, but with force.

They do not break up white supremacist marches.

They do not raid the homes of corrupt CEOs.

They do not crack down on human rights violations in corporate offices.

But they will come for you if you disrupt the system.

They protect wealth, not life.

They enforce obedience, not justice.

They safeguard power, not the people.

And every time history moves forward, they are there to drag it back.

Policing Cannot Be Reformed—It Must Be Replaced

Every time police kill an unarmed citizen, the answer is the same: reform.

More training.

More oversight.

More funding.

But more funding just buys them more weapons. More training just makes them better at justifying their violence. More oversight means more paperwork, not less brutality.

The system is not broken. It is functioning exactly as designed.

You cannot train an overseer to be merciful.

You cannot teach an enforcer to be just.

You cannot fix a system that does not see you as human.

And the truth is simple:

They will ride until they are stopped.

And they will only be stopped when the people make them irrelevant.

"Hands Up, Don't…."

I see the red and blue lights flickering in my mirror,

feel the pit in my stomach drop,

pulse hammering before the sirens even scream.

I know this drill.

Ten and two. Eyes forward. No sudden moves.

Don't reach for the phone. Don't check the glove box.

Don't give them a reason.

Not that they need one.

I take a breath.

Then another.

It doesn't help.

A shadow approaches.

Heavy boots against pavement.

Hand already on his holster.

He is ready.

For what, I don't know.

I pray I never find out.

Knuckle taps against glass, harder than it needs to be.

Like he's knocking on a coffin.

Mine.

I roll the window down slow.

Not too slow—don't seem hesitant.

Not too fast—don't seem aggressive.

Every second is a calculation, every movement a risk.

"License and registration."

My voice cracks as I speak,

as if fear is an admission of guilt.

"It's in my glove box," I say,

because I need him to know where my hands are going

before I move, before he moves,

before this becomes another name on a long list

that America will pretend to grieve.

He nods once,

but I see it—

the shift in his stance,

the way his fingers tighten around the grip of his gun.

As if my seatbelted body

in a car I pay for

on a street I have every right to drive

is suddenly a threat.

I move slow.

I don't reach—I ease.

I don't grab—I lift.

The envelope is in my hand now.

He flinches.

I stop breathing.

"Step out of the car."

My stomach twists.

I know what comes next.

I know that "step out" could mean I never step back in.

That my next move determines whether I make it home

or whether my mother gets a phone call

telling her the son she raised is now a statistic.

"Is there a problem, officer?"

There shouldn't be.

But we both know there is.

He yanks the door open before I can,

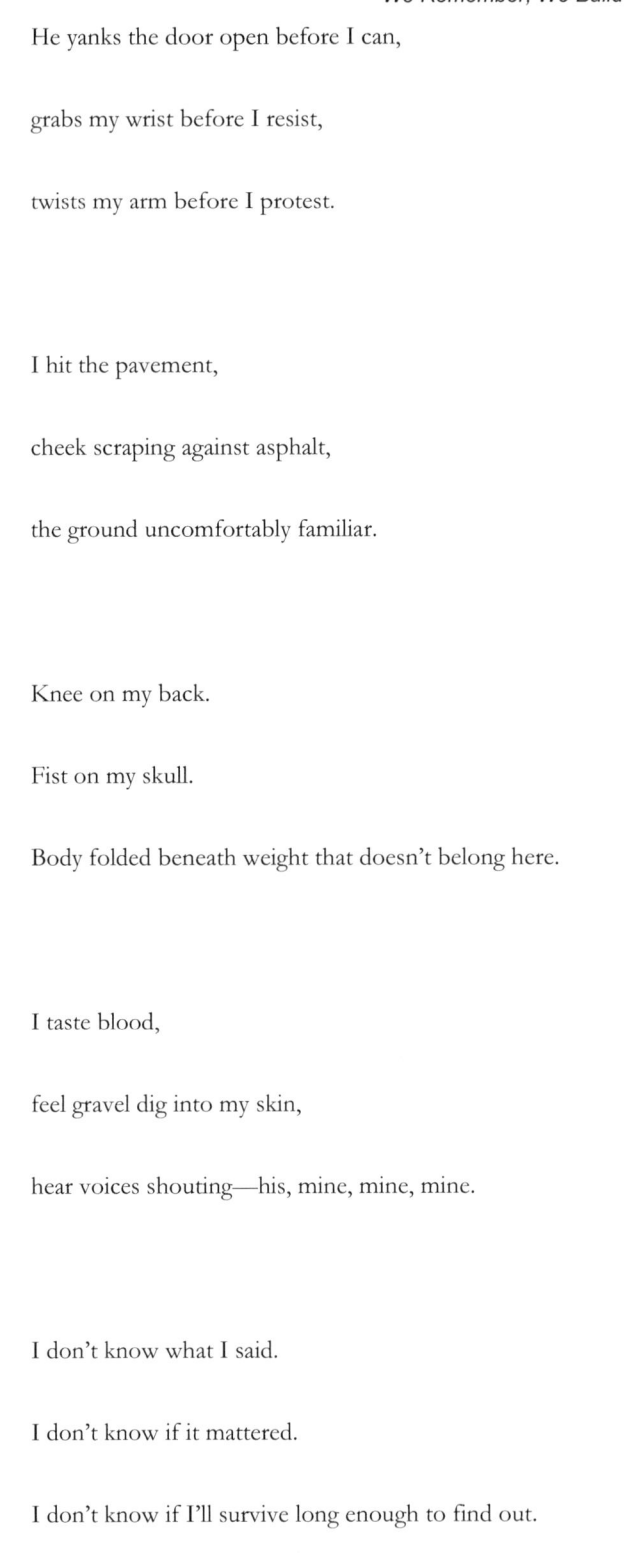

grabs my wrist before I resist,

twists my arm before I protest.

I hit the pavement,

cheek scraping against asphalt,

the ground uncomfortably familiar.

Knee on my back.

Fist on my skull.

Body folded beneath weight that doesn't belong here.

I taste blood,

feel gravel dig into my skin,

hear voices shouting—his, mine, mine, mine.

I don't know what I said.

I don't know if it mattered.

I don't know if I'll survive long enough to find out.

My arms twist behind me.

My wrists scream.

Metal bites flesh—tight, then tighter.

I am contained now.

Secured.

Restrained.

And still,

he presses down.

Still,

he holds his weight against me.

Still,

his hands crush the breath from my body.

"Please," I whisper.

Or maybe I don't.

Maybe the words never make it past my lips.

Maybe they never do.

A crowd gathers.

Phone cameras rise.

Someone yells,

but no one moves.

Because they know.

Because we all know.

Because we've seen this before,

and we will see it again.

I wish I could say I remember what happened next.

I wish I could say I walked away.

I wish I could say I stood up.

But the lights blur.

The sirens drown.

The world fades.

And the last thing I hear

is the weight of him

crushing the air from my lungs.

Somewhere, my mother's phone is ringing.

Somewhere, my name is already becoming a hashtag.

Somewhere, America is watching this happen.

Again.

Again.

Again.

Masters of the Modern Age

How Political Sponsors Own the System

They don't need to stand on podiums.

They don't need to debate on live TV.

They don't have to kiss babies, shake hands, or smile for cameras.

Because they already own the stage, the candidates, and the script.

These are the masters behind the curtain. The ones who fund campaigns, shape policies, and control the decisions made in city halls, statehouses, and on Capitol Hill.

They don't run for office.

They buy it.

And once they do, the game is rigged from the top.

The Puppet Show: When Money Moves the Mouths of Power

Every law, every policy, every budget passed in this country begins with a simple question:

Who paid for it to exist?

Politicians don't serve the public—they serve donors, corporations, and political sponsors who ensure that their interests are protected above all.

- A corporation donates to a campaign.
- That candidate wins.
- The corporation receives a tax break, a deregulation, or a government contract.
- The cycle repeats.

This is not governance. This is ownership.

And while the public argues over parties and personalities, the masters behind the scenes remain untouched. Their goals are simple:

- Protect profit.
- Weaken resistance.
- Silence dissent.
- Preserve the system that keeps them at the top.

Democracy? That's the costume.

The money decides who gets the mic.

Legislation for Sale: How Corporations Write the Rules

In a true democracy, laws are written by elected officials to reflect the will of the people.

In America, many laws are written by private interest groups.

Take ALEC—the American Legislative Exchange Council. A corporate-funded organization that literally writes bills and hands them to state lawmakers.

- "Stand Your Ground" laws? Written and pushed by ALEC.
- Voter suppression tactics? Backed by ALEC.
- Corporate tax breaks and environmental rollbacks? Their fingerprints are all over them.

And ALEC is just one name in a long list of puppet master:

- Big Pharma, controlling health care policy to protect sky-high prices.
- Oil and gas companies, ensuring that green energy bills die quietly in committee.
- Defense contractors, feeding endless wars to keep the checks coming.

These are the real authors of legislation.

Politicians just sign their names.

Citizens United: The Legalization of Corruption

In 2010, the Supreme Court made a decision that opened the floodgates: Citizens United v. FEC.

The ruling said that corporations have the same free speech rights as people.

That money equals speech.

And that there can be no limit to how much a corporation or wealthy individual can spend to influence an election.

In other words, bribery was rebranded as campaign finance.

Now, billionaires don't just influence elections.

They purchase them outright.

They create Super PACs.

They buy ad time, public opinion, and political silence.

They make sure that every viable candidate, no matter the party, understands the rules:

Don't bite the hand that funds you.

And the people?

They get promises.

They get slogans.

They get speeches that sound like revolution but deliver nothing.

The Master's Voice: Lobbyists and Legislative Capture

Once a politician is elected, the puppeteering doesn't stop—it deepens.

Lobbyists flood congressional offices with offers, data, drafted bills, and checks.

They sit at the table while the people wait in line outside.

Lobbyists for the private prison industry ensure that sentencing laws stay harsh.

Lobbyists for weapons manufacturers ensure the U.S. stays armed to the teeth.

Lobbyists for tech giants block regulation to protect their monopolies.

This is not influence.

This is control.

And every year, billions are spent to make sure legislation serves the few—

even when it harms the many.

Even when it kills.

Who Pays the Price?

While the donors reap profits, the people pay in poverty, violence, and despair.

- Communities go without clean water because utility contracts were sold off for profit.
- Public schools crumble while private charter donors cash in.
- Neighborhoods are overpoliced, not for safety, but because law enforcement unions are powerful funders.
- Medical bankruptcies continue while health insurance companies keep their profits protected by law.

This is not policy failure.

It is the system working exactly as it was bought to work.

No One is Coming to Save Us

There will be no hero candidate.

No perfect politician.

No reform from within.

Because the game is not broken.

It is functioning exactly as the sponsors designed it.

And the only way to win a rigged game

is to flip the table.

Until then, the masters will keep pulling strings.

The puppets will keep pretending to serve.

And the people will be told to vote harder, pray louder, wait longer—

for a change that was never meant to come.

"Strings Attached"

I get up before the sun.

Bus comes at six.

Shoes still damp from yesterday's shift,

lunch packed in reused grocery bags,

uniform pressed just enough to pass.

I wipe my baby's face with one hand,

sign a past-due bill with the other,

kiss my mom on the cheek

as she gets the kids ready

so I can go work a job

that still can't carry us all.

They say I'm "essential."

But I can't afford an emergency.

Not a flat tire.

Not a prescription.

Not a sick day.

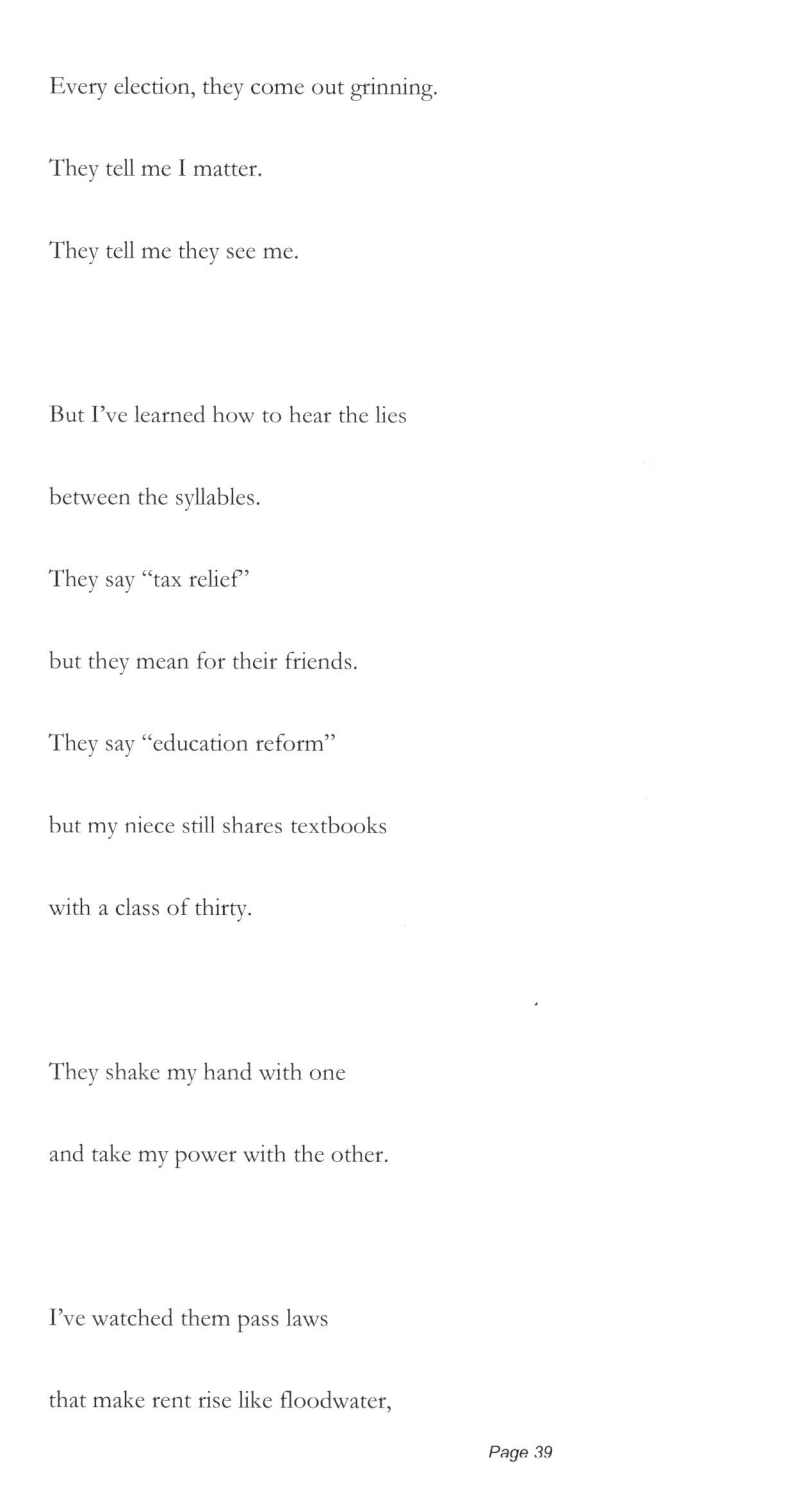

Every election, they come out grinning.

They tell me I matter.

They tell me they see me.

But I've learned how to hear the lies

between the syllables.

They say "tax relief"

but they mean for their friends.

They say "education reform"

but my niece still shares textbooks

with a class of thirty.

They shake my hand with one

and take my power with the other.

I've watched them pass laws

that make rent rise like floodwater,

that gut programs I used to rely on

just to say the budget's balanced.

They tell me to get involved—

but don't fund the bus routes

to the polling places they hide.

They say "justice."

I see prisons being traded on Wall Street.

They say "opportunity."

I see student loans breaking the spines

of kids just trying to get free.

I stock shelves.

I fix engines.

I clean offices

where men in suits make decisions

that keep me tired,

and them rich.

But I'm not blind.

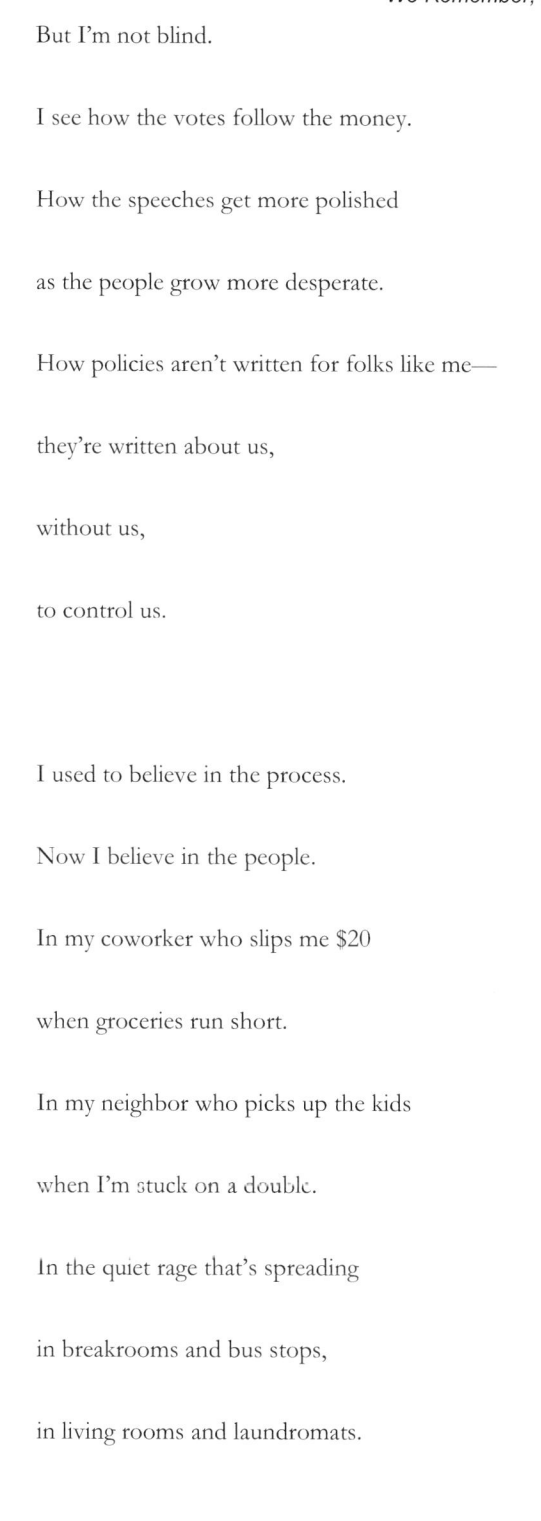

I see how the votes follow the money.

How the speeches get more polished

as the people grow more desperate.

How policies aren't written for folks like me—

they're written about us,

without us,

to control us.

I used to believe in the process.

Now I believe in the people.

In my coworker who slips me $20

when groceries run short.

In my neighbor who picks up the kids

when I'm stuck on a double.

In the quiet rage that's spreading

in breakrooms and bus stops,

in living rooms and laundromats.

We may not sit behind the curtains.

But we feel every pull of the string.

And we've had enough.

We've been the hands that built it,

the backs that held it up,

the silence that kept it running.

But silence grows teeth.

And backs break into fists.

And hands—

hands remember how to tear things down.

So keep pulling your strings.

Keep hiding behind your curtains.

We're not asking anymore.

We're coming to burn the whole stage down.

Labor in Chains

How Workers and Children Remain Enslaved to Capitalism

They start us young.

Before we learn how to ask why, we're taught how to sit still. Before we can think critically, we're told to follow instructions. By the time we're old enough to dream, we're too conditioned to question who benefits from the way things are.

This isn't education.

This is training. Conditioning. Indoctrination.

The classroom is the first factory.

The desk is the first workstation.

The bell is the first alarm clock.

The curriculum is the first manual on how to survive—not succeed—in a system designed to keep us useful, not free.

The School-to-Workforce Pipeline: Designed for Obedience

From an early age, children—especially those in working-class, Black, and brown communities—are placed on a track that mirrors the very structure of industrial labor:

- Bell schedules teach compliance to external control.
- Standardized testing enforces uniformity and rewards conformity.
- Zero-tolerance policies condition children to associate mistakes with punishment, not growth.
- Curricula often erase histories of resistance, replacing them with sanitized versions of American exceptionalism.

We are not taught to ask:

- Who owns what?
- Why does poverty exist?
- What does it mean to be free?

We are taught to obey. To produce. To compete. To internalize scarcity.

Education, in capitalist America, is not liberation. It is preparation for labor in a system that demands your body, your time, and your silence.

The Curriculum of Capitalism

What is knowledge without power? In many schools, students memorize facts with no context, no application, and no connection to the world they live in. But what they do learn—often implicitly—is their place in the structure:

- That "success" means individual achievement, not collective uplift.
- That "hard work" always pays off, even if the system is rigged.
- That if you struggle, it's your fault—not the fault of a world that was never built with you in mind.

Meanwhile, arts programs are cut. Critical thinking is labeled as disruptive. Alternative worldviews are discouraged. Teachers are underpaid, overworked, and stripped of autonomy.

This is not accidental. This is how capitalism ensures a steady stream of workers who won't revolt. The schools don't just underdeliver—they are actively participating in the production of compliant labor.

From Classroom to Clock-In

By the time students graduate, they are ready for the next phase: labor. Not fulfillment. Not freedom. Labor.

And the rules are the same:

- Obey authority.
- Ask permission to rest.
- Produce more than you are paid.
- Be grateful you're employed.
- Don't ask why your CEO makes more in a day than you make in a year.

Whether it's a warehouse or a cubicle, a fast food chain or a hospital, the machinery of capitalism does not care about the person inside the uniform. It only cares that you show up, shut up, and keep the engine running.

Work is not about value. It's about control. And the chains are tighter when you've been trained to wear them since childhood.

Poverty as Policy

Let's be clear: poverty is not the result of laziness, bad choices, or lack of talent. Poverty is a product. It is engineered by a system that thrives on imbalance.

If everyone had what they needed, who would clean the billionaires' houses?

If wages were fair, who would work 60 hours a week for food and rent?

If education were liberating, who would accept a lifetime of debt just to survive?

Capitalism doesn't just allow poverty. It requires it.

And both children and workers are kept in place by this design—chasing dreams the system never intends to fulfill.

The Weight We Carry Across Generations

The cruelty of the system isn't just economic—it's emotional.

How many children are told they're lazy for not conforming to schools that do not recognize their brilliance?

How many workers believe they are failing, not realizing they are set up to never get ahead?

How many generations of people internalize powerlessness because that's the only version of success they've ever been shown?

This is how capitalism steals more than time. It steals identity, confidence, and imagination. It punishes the bold and rewards the obedient. It teaches us not to ask for freedom, but to survive inside confinement.

But Cracks Are Forming

This system is not invincible. People are waking up.

- Teachers are walking out of classrooms, not for pay alone, but for dignity—for smaller class sizes, culturally relevant curricula, and the end of school-to-prison pipelines.
- Students are organizing against book bans, budget cuts, and policies that dehumanize them.
- Workers are unionizing, striking, reclaiming their labor. From Amazon warehouses to Starbucks counters to public service offices, the refusal to be silent is growing.
- Entire communities are building models of mutual aid, cooperative economics, and liberation schools outside the system's grip.

These acts are not small. They are proof that the machine can be disrupted.

That people are not property, that labor is not submission, and that education is not obedience unless we allow it to be.

Breaking the Chains Means Redefining Value

The first act of resistance is recognizing the lie.

- That you were not born to be someone's labor.
- That your worth is not tied to your output.
- That children are not future workers—they are future visionaries, artists, organizers, builders of a new world.

But that world can't grow from chains.

It must be built from freedom, from rest, from education rooted in truth.

From labor that serves life, not profit.

The Reckoning Is Coming

The system continues because we keep showing up.

But every time a worker walks out,

every time a student questions the lesson,

every time a parent demands more,

the chains rattle.

And when we rise—together, organized, unafraid—

the machinery will not know how to run without us.

Because it was never built to be just.

It was built to extract.

And we were never meant to live this way.

We were meant to be free.

"First Bell"

Mama says I'm ready.
She packed my lunch in foil love,
braided my hair like roots that hold,
kissed my cheek and whispered,
"Be brave, baby. But be careful too."

I've been learning at home since I could talk—
how to name the clouds,
how to count the cracks in the sidewalk,
how to tell truth from noise
when grown-ups don't say what they mean.

At home, I ask why
and someone always answers.
Even when they're tired.
Even when the answer is hard.

At home, I build cities out of cardboard,
write songs on napkins,
paint suns with too many rays
because I like it that way.

But today, the sky feels smaller.
My shoes feel too new.
And the backpack is heavy,
not with books—
but with something I can't name.

Mama holds my hand until the gate.
I see the building—

big, gray, square.

It doesn't look like a place that dreams.

Inside, children sit in lines.

They whisper like they're afraid to be loud.

A bell rings.

Everyone moves at once.

No one asks why.

The teacher is kind.

But she talks like a timer is running.

Her eyes flick to the clock

like it's her boss.

We talk about numbers, letters,

but not why the boy next to me has holes in his shoes.

Not why the janitor doesn't smile.

Not why the flag hangs high

but the kid with brown skin gets sent to the office

for asking the same question I just did.

We sit still.

We raise our hands.

We wait for permission

to use the bathroom,

to speak,

to think.

And I wonder—

what happens if I don't raise my hand?

What happens if I draw the sun with too many rays again?

Will they tell me I'm wrong

for seeing more than they taught me to see?

What if my questions come out too loud?

Will they think I'm trouble,

or will they remember

that before I got here,

I was already whole?

Mama told me school would help me grow.

But I feel smaller in my chair.

I feel the room bending me into shape.

I feel myself folding to fit.

And I don't want to forget

the way I dreamed before the bell.

I don't want to trade wonder for worksheets,

or courage for compliance.

So I tuck my questions deep in my pocket,

carry them like treasure

through the rest of the day.

And I promise myself—

if they won't let me speak them here,

I'll speak them somewhere louder.

Somewhere brighter.

Somewhere free.

PART TWO

THE BREAKING POINT

How resistance rises and the system fights back

The War on Truth

How Media and Misinformation Keep the Chains Tight

In a country built on stolen land, unpaid labor, and the illusion of meritocracy, the most dangerous weapon has never been the gun. It's the story.

Because if you can control the story,

you can control the people who live inside it.

And that's exactly what the system does—through a network of corporate media, social platforms, and state-sanctioned disinformation, it shapes not only what we believe but what we're allowed to believe.

Media Is Not a Mirror—It's a Weapon

The American media landscape presents itself as neutral—fair, balanced, objective. But that's a lie told so often it's become a cornerstone of the system itself.

- Just six corporations control about 90% of what Americans watch, read, and hear: Comcast, Disney, AT&T (Warner Bros), Paramount, News Corp (Fox), and Sony.
- These corporations have deep ties to banks, defense contractors, pharmaceutical giants, and fossil fuel industries.
- Their survival depends on maintaining the power structures that keep their investors rich and the public docile.

This is why wars are sold to us like products.

This is why poverty is criminalized, but wealth hoarding is celebrated.

This is why uprisings are called riots, but generational exploitation isn't called theft.

The media does not reflect reality.

It reflects what the ruling class needs reality to look like in order to stay on top.

Propaganda in a Suit and Tie

They no longer need to burn books or shut down newspapers.

They simply need to make sure truth is never centered—never made visible enough to matter.

- During the Civil Rights era, mainstream media often painted Martin Luther King Jr. as a dangerous radical. Only after his assassination did they reframe him as a harmless dreamer.
- COINTELPRO worked hand-in-hand with media outlets to discredit and destroy Black leaders like Fred Hampton and Assata Shakur—flooding the public with fear and misinformation.
- In 2003, every major network repeated the government's lie about Iraq's "weapons of mass destruction," manufacturing consent for a war that killed hundreds of thousands.

This isn't bias.

It's complicity.

The media doesn't just report on power—it protects it.

And when truth threatens power, they bury it under headlines that are more comfortable, more profitable, and more forgettable.

Misinformation Is Not Mistake—It's Method

The system doesn't fear lies. It needs them.

Because lies buy time—time for laws to pass, wars to be funded, and dissent to be silenced.

In recent years:

- QAnon conspiracies spread through social media while tech companies raked in ad dollars.
- Misinformation about COVID-19 killed thousands, while networks profited from fear and outrage.
- Voter suppression was disguised as "election integrity" and repeated across platforms with no accountability.

And in the chaos, the public is too overwhelmed to act.

When no one knows what's real, no one knows where to fight.

This is not confusion.

This is control.

The Algorithm Is the New Overseer

Social media promised democratization of truth—but it became another machine of suppression.

- Activist accounts are flagged, shadowbanned, or deleted.
- Truth-tellers are drowned under a flood of irrelevant content, clickbait, and digital noise.
- Platforms like Meta, X, and YouTube profit from surveillance, while giving corporations and governments access to manipulate global narratives.

What's trending isn't what matters.

It's what's allowed.

And what's allowed is what keeps the system intact.

Narrative Policing: Who Gets to Speak?

A single police officer's death is national news.

Thousands of people brutalized by police become a statistic.

A white mass shooter is framed as mentally ill.

A Black child with a toy gun is framed as a threat.

Colonizers are called "explorers."

Revolutionaries are called "thugs."

Billionaires are called "job creators."

Poor people are called "lazy."

This isn't about language.

It's about legitimacy.

The media decides who gets to be human.

Who gets to be heard.

Who gets to be believed.

Truth Tellers Are Silenced Without a Sound

You don't always need a bullet to kill a voice.

Sometimes you just need a lack of coverage.

- Assata Shakur lives in exile while most Americans don't even know her name.
- Whistleblowers like Chelsea Manning and Edward Snowden were imprisoned or exiled for revealing the government's crimes.
- Colin Kaepernick was erased from professional football for kneeling silently—while talking heads flooded screens with rage about his "disrespect."

The system makes examples of truth-tellers.

Not to kill them—

but to kill our willingness to speak.

When the Story Is Controlled, So Is the Future

If we only know what they teach us,

If we only hear what they want us to hear,

If we only speak what's safe to say—

then we're not just silenced.

We're enslaved to a reality that isn't real.

Because truth is not just about facts.

It's about direction.

It's about power.

It's about liberation.

Reclaiming the Narrative Is Revolutionary

This war on truth is not just fought on screens. It's fought in our minds, our timelines, our classrooms, our conversations.

To fight back:

- We must build independent platforms, radical media, and local storytelling networks.
- We must question every source, every spin, every silence.
- We must amplify our voices louder than their algorithms allow.

Because when people stop believing the story,

they start writing a new one.

And the system knows:

once the people know the truth,

the chains start to break.

Every Headline a Chain, Every Silence a Lock

Breonna Taylor's Civil Rights Were Violated by Ex-Louisville Officer, Jury Determines

Baton Rouge Police Accused of 'Unconscionable' Abuse in 'Brave Cave'

Black Family Fights Railroad's Eminent Domain Claim on Ancestral Land

Why the Court Hit the Brakes on School Desegregation

Gaza Protesters Sue UCLA for Civil Rights Violations After 'Brutal Attack' in 2024

Law Enforcement Killed Cop City Protestor Tortuguita. Now Their Parents Are Suing

Chicago Schools' Bid to Boost Black Student Achievement Draws Legal Challenge

Things to Know About the Federal Investigation Into the Memphis Police Department

Anti-DEI Crusade in U.S. Allows Discrimination — Human Rights Watch

'Like a War Zone': Emory University Grapples With Fallout From Police Response to Protest

And still they wonder why we rage, why we rise, why we never forget.

Silencing the Fire

How the System Crushes Revolution

They don't wait until the revolution arrives.

They kill it while it's still a whisper.

Before the march becomes a movement.

Before the organizer becomes a leader.

Before the people believe they have the right to say no.

This system doesn't panic when a law is challenged.

It panics when the powerless begin to imagine power of their own.

And that's when it moves—not to argue, not to reform—

but to erase.

Because nothing threatens the empire more than those who refuse to serve it quietly.

And so, across decades, across state lines, across continents, it reaches out with the same goal:

"Silence the fire before it spreads."

Revolution Is Always Met With Repression

The United States has never tolerated a clear-eyed, loud-voiced challenge to its order.

When people rise with strategy, solidarity, and truth—the state responds with every tool it has:

- Surveillance
- Infiltration
- Misinformation
- Arrest
- Character assassination
- Displacement
- And in too many cases—murder

This is not theory.

This is history.

And it's still happening.

They Fear What Cannot Be Controlled

From slavery to civil rights, from labor uprisings to antiwar movements, this country has consistently sought to destroy those who dared to imagine another world:

- Denmark Vesey, executed for daring to plan freedom.
- Fred Hampton, drugged and shot in his bed at 21 for feeding, educating, and organizing the Black poor.
- Martin Luther King Jr., vilified for opposing capitalism and militarism, assassinated once he began naming the root of inequality.
- Assata Shakur, falsely convicted, forced into exile, her image demonized while her truth was erased.

Their crime wasn't violence.

Their crime was vision.

They weren't trying to burn the system down.

They were trying to build something better.

And that's what power cannot tolerate.

COINTELPRO: The Blueprint for Silencing

Between 1956 and 1971, the FBI ran a covert operation called COINTELPRO (Counterintelligence Program). Its goal?

"Prevent the rise of a Black messiah."

It did more than spy. It:

- Infiltrated movements
- Pitted leaders against one another
- Spread lies through newspapers
- Blackmailed and harassed families
- Falsified documents
- Arrested revolutionaries on fabricated charges

And when destruction wasn't enough—they killed.

They made examples of those who dared to unify the working class, cross racial lines, or build self-sustaining communities.

This wasn't policing. It was warfare.

And its tactics didn't end—they just changed uniforms.

Bombs and Borders: The Fire They Tried to Erase

In 1985, the city of Philadelphia dropped a literal bomb on a home occupied by Black liberation group MOVE—killing 11 people, including 5 children, and burning down 61 surrounding homes.

No one was held accountable.

The message was clear:

"We will destroy everything to silence what we fear."

And the fire crossed borders.

The U.S. government also targeted Puerto Rican independence fighters like Lolita Lebrón, who spent decades in prison, and Oscar López Rivera, who was held for 35 years—longer than many convicted of violent crimes.

The FBI maintained secret surveillance files on thousands of Puerto Rican activists and journalists—merely for demanding freedom from colonial rule.

This wasn't about protecting peace.

It was about preserving control.

Even the idea of self-determination was a threat.

The Fire Didn't Die—It's Still Imprisoned

The system may rewrite history, but some fires still burn—locked behind bars.

- Mumia Abu-Jamal, former Black Panther and journalist, has been imprisoned for over 40 years after a trial riddled with bias and misconduct.
- Leonard Peltier, Indigenous rights activist, remains incarcerated despite international outcry and zero physical evidence tying him to the crime.
- Countless political prisoners from the 60s, 70s, and 80s sit in aging prison cells, abandoned by the country they tried to change.

Their sentences are not about guilt.

They're about sending a message:

"We saw your fire. We caged it."

Media: The Silent Co-Conspirator

The killing doesn't stop with bullets or bars—it continues with narrative control.

- Fred Hampton is rarely taught in schools.
- Assata Shakur's story is flattened into fugitive status.

- Angela Davis's mugshot circulates more than her scholarship.
- BLM leaders are treated as grifters, not organizers.

Even peaceful resistance is demonized.

Protest becomes "chaos."

Community defense becomes "terrorism."

Radical thought becomes "hate speech."

And the public is trained to look away.

The System's Final Weapon: Fear

The silencing isn't just external—it gets inside us.

- We hesitate to speak.
- We hold back in meetings.
- We shrink when the moment calls us to rise.

Because we remember.

Because we've seen what happens.

Because we're told in a thousand quiet ways:

"That fire you carry? Don't let it grow too loud."

And so we dim.

And so we burn quietly.

And that is how they win—not with force alone, but with our permission.

But the Fire Doesn't Belong to Them

What they never understand is this:

The fire was never theirs to extinguish.

It lives in the grief of mothers who bury their sons.

It lives in the hunger of workers who can't make rent.

It lives in the rage of children who ask, "Why is the world like this?"

It lives in the poetry, the protest, the paintings, the prayers.

And no matter how many cages they build,

how many names they erase,

how many headlines they rewrite—

fire spreads.

It only takes one breath.

One hand on another's shoulder.

One whisper that becomes a chorus.

And then—

They'll remember what happens when the people stop being afraid.

They'll remember that fire does not beg to burn.

It just does.

The Pulpit Ain't the People

I watched her step up to the podium,
the same sister who once cried beside me at the altar.
We shared pews, passed communion plates,
held hands when the choir sang,
"Break every chain."

Now she speaks in the language of politics,
but I can still hear the scripture under her voice—
twisted now,
shaped to serve men in suits
who never knew how to pray with both hands open.

Her dress is pressed, her smile rehearsed,
her words dipped in polished poison:
"Order."
"Public safety."
"Responsible reform."
I've heard those words before—
right before the riot gear,
right before the bulldozers,
right before the budget cuts
and the press conference that called us unruly.

I wanted to believe she remembered.
The mother with three jobs.
The boy whose name we had to bury.
The elder who got evicted while still shouting hallelujah.

But power fits some people like a borrowed robe.
And now she wears it like it was made for her.

I clapped politely,

but my hands felt wrong.

My fire burned in my chest—

not out of jealousy,

but betrayal.

Because when she speaks now,

it isn't prophecy.

It's policy.

And policy don't save souls.

It sells them.

They call it progress,

but I see the chains polished, not broken.

I see the altar turned into a stage.

And I see my sister,

no longer lifting up the people—

but pressing us down with the same boots

she used to pray against.

But me—

I still carry that fire.

I still believe in sacred rebellion.

I still believe the God of the oppressed

don't bless ballots soaked in silence.

Don't smile on speeches crafted to quiet the cry.

So while she walks carpeted halls,

I walk cracked sidewalks

with the mothers,

with the fed-up saints,

with the children who never got a podium.

And when I sing now,

it's not a hymn—it's a warning.

A prayer with teeth.

A blaze at the gate.

Because the revolution is still holy.

And I—

I still burn.

The Myth of Reform
Why Change Can't Come from the System That Enslaved Us

Every generation is offered the same pacifier:

"Be patient. Change is coming."

And every generation who waits for it finds themselves asking the same question:

"Why does the system we're asked to trust always protect the ones we're fighting against?"

Because reform is not a promise.

It's a performance.

A distraction.

A temporary shift in shape—never in power.

It's the myth that a structure built on our backs will somehow save us when it's done using us.

But how can we reform a system that was never broken—just working exactly as it was designed?

The System Was Never Designed to Be Just

Slavery wasn't a glitch. It was a foundation.

The Three-Fifths Compromise, the Electoral College, and the Constitution itself were constructed to protect power—not to share it.

Policing didn't evolve from law enforcement. It was born from slave patrols, designed to hunt down those who tried to escape.

The criminal justice system didn't fall into mass incarceration—it redirected the labor force after the abolition of slavery through Black Codes, vagrancy laws, and convict leasing.

Prisons, public housing, welfare, and even schools have always been used to regulate labor, contain unrest, and punish the poor for surviving.

And when we fight back, the system doesn't dismantle itself.

It morphs.

It uses the language of change to protect the structure of control.

Hope Has Always Been Offered—And Then Denied

We've seen the cycle over and over:

- In the Reconstruction Era, we were promised freedom, land, and full participation. What we got was lynching, Jim Crow, and mass disenfranchisement.
- In the Civil Rights Era, we were offered desegregation and the Voting Rights Act—only to be met with redlining, white flight, and the War on Drugs.
- In the Obama era, we were told change had come. But under his presidency, the Ferguson uprising erupted, the 1994 Crime Bill remained untouched, and Wall Street was rescued while Black communities drowned.

Even today, "diverse" faces are placed in high positions—judges, mayors, police chiefs, even Vice Presidents—and we're told that's victory.

But what good is representation if the system beneath them remains untouched?

When Reform Feels Like a Lie You Wanted to Believe

We all wanted to believe it could be different.

We wanted to believe that progress was real.

That if we voted the right way, marched peacefully, educated ourselves, trusted the system—we could fix it.

Because hope is holy.

Because struggle makes us weary.

Because believing in reform makes the fight feel lighter—like we might not have to burn everything down.

But then you look around…

You remember:

- The schools in your neighborhood still underfunded
- The child who died in a prison cell
- The officer who killed and kept his badge
- The program that sounded good but changed nothing
- The bills passed in name but never funded, never enforced
- The jobs created but not protected
- The housing that costs more than your breath
- The way they promised peace—but never delivered justice

And it hits you:

They knew. They always knew.

The reform wasn't meant to work. It was meant to keep us waiting.

The Nonprofit Industrial Complex: Compassion in Chains

Even revolution gets repackaged.

The system has learned how to swallow resistance whole—and spit it back out as paperwork.

This is how the nonprofit industrial complex works:

- It takes raw, urgent movements and makes them "grant-ready."
- It offers jobs to organizers—but with terms and conditions.
- It creates community leaders who have platforms—but no freedom to name the real enemy.
- It turns calls for abolition into "dialogues," demands for land into "partnerships," protests into panels.

And most of the time, it's run by people who mean well.

People who believe they're doing the work.

People who started on the front lines and got pulled into offices where their language changed and their fire got managed.

That's the cruelty of it:

It doesn't silence the people by force. It gives them titles. Budgets. Conferences. Deadlines.

And soon, the revolution starts wearing a name badge.

The Reformers Who Block the Door

Then come the figures who look like us—who speak our dialect, quote our scriptures, know our pain—but stand at the gate.

They are the politicians, appointees, nonprofit CEOs, campaign strategists, school board members, foundation directors.

They take meetings.

They calm tempers.

They ask for trust.

But behind them?

The same system.

The same funding.

The same outcomes.

They are not always malicious.

Sometimes, they truly think they can change it from within.

But when the time comes to choose between protecting people or protecting institutions—the people are too often sacrificed.

And worse:

They tell us the fire is too loud.

They ask us to wait.

They beg us not to burn the thing that's killing us.

Reform Is the System's Favorite Trick

It always begins the same way:

- A crisis exposes the truth.
- People flood the streets.
- The nation pretends to listen.
- Leaders offer a reform to quiet the storm.

But that reform is always limited, vague, or impossible to enforce.

It's carefully designed to appease without restructuring.

After George Floyd's murder, what did we get?

- A surge of public apologies.
- A few murals.
- Some body cameras.
- A bill that stalled before it passed.

But the police budget grew.

The brutality didn't stop.

And the system that killed George kept on breathing like nothing had changed.

Reform is not transformation.

It's the sound of power saying,

"We heard you. Now sit down."

Historical Reforms That Maintained Oppression

Let's be honest.

- The Emancipation Proclamation freed the enslaved—then Black Codes and convict leasing re-enslaved them.
- The 13th Amendment abolished slavery "except as punishment for crime." That exception built the modern prison state.
- The Civil Rights Act ended legal segregation—then redlining, underfunded schools, and policing filled the gap.
- Desegregation was promised—then undone by white flight, charter schools, and court rollbacks.
- Voting rights were expanded—then gutted by Shelby v. Holder, voter ID laws, and gerrymandering.
- Even reparations commissions have led to studies, not solutions.

The system survives by adapting.

It doesn't retreat.

It rebrands.

We Are Not Broken for Feeling Betrayed

If you've ever felt like the victory was hollow,
like the bill didn't go far enough,
like the politician you believed in betrayed the movement—
you are not broken.
You're awake.

Reform doesn't fail because we didn't try hard enough.
It fails because the system was built to survive our demands—not fulfill them.
And when that truth hits you,
when your hope turns heavy,
that's not the end.

That's the beginning of clarity.

This Is Not Cynicism. This Is Clarity.
Believing in revolution doesn't mean giving up on hope.
It means redefining hope.
Hope is not begging.
Hope is not waiting.
Hope is what we build with our own hands when we stop asking for permission.

Reform says: "Let us fix it."
Revolution says: "We'll build something new."
Reform says: "Be patient."
Revolution says: "The time is now."
And the people are waking up.

"What's Gonna Change?"

"They finally charged him," Harold said,
his voice low, watching the screen.
Another police shooting.
Another press conference.
Same tie. Same flag.
Same tired promise.

Miss Thelma didn't look up.
She just stirred her tea slow.
"I seen that before," she said.
"Every few years they throw us one.
Just enough to keep folks calm."

Harold shook his head.
"I don't know, Thelma.
Feels different this time."
She chuckled soft,
not mocking—just tired.
"You said that last time too."

They sat quiet for a moment,
TV flickering in the corner
like a bad memory trying to be new.

"You remember when we thought
the right law would fix it?" he asked.
"Marchin' felt like somethin'.
Voting felt like power."

"I remember," Thelma said.

"I remember feelin' proud.

Hope was heavy back then.

But we carried it."

She looked out the window—

past the trees,

past the gate,

to where some kids were playin'

with jump ropes and chalk on the sidewalk.

Their laughter cut through the still air.

She smiled,

just barely.

"You think they'll be the ones?" he asked.

She didn't answer right away.

Just watched.

"I think if we keep waitin' on these folks to do right,

those kids gon' be sittin' where we are,

askin' the same damn questions."

Harold leaned back.

"That's what hurts most, ain't it?"

"Mm-hmm."

She took a sip.

"But I tell you what," Thelma said,

finally turning toward him.

"I done stopped lookin' to them.

Started lookin' to us.

Started thinkin' maybe all this time,

we been tryin' to fix somethin'

that wasn't built for us to live in."

Harold nodded.

Didn't speak for a while.

Then:

"You're right.

Maybe fixin' ain't what we need."

He glanced out the window too now.

"They just need to grow up knowin' better.

Knowin' they can build their own thing."

Thelma smiled again,

this time with her whole face.

"Now that," she said,

"sounds like somethin' worth livin' for."

The Boiling Point
When the People Refuse to Bend

You can stretch a people for only so long before the thread snaps.

You can bury truth under lies, drown voices in silence, and pacify rage with promises—

but sooner or later, the weight of it all meets its match.

That match is the people.

Not just the organizers or the leaders.

Not just the ones with microphones or media coverage.

But the mother who's had enough.

The worker who can't breathe.

The child who learns too early how justice doesn't come.

At some point, the people stop asking.

They stop bending.

They rise—not because they want to destroy, but because they want to live.

Rebellion Is Not the Breakdown—It's the Refusal to Break

They will call it chaos.

They will call it lawlessness.

They will flash images of burning buildings and angry chants.

But they won't show what came before:

- The housing denied
- The hands cuffed without reason.
- The ballot boxes purged.
- The grocery stores closing.
- The hospitals refusing care.
- The jobs paying pennies.
- The generations told to wait, and wait, and wait

What the system calls a riot

is often the last prayer of the unheard.

What the media calls violent

is often the consequence of silence.

You can only be polite with your pain for so long

before your grief grows legs

and walks out into the street.

History Always Reaches a Boiling Point

This country has always waited until the people force its hand:

- Enslaved Africans burned plantations and escaped north.
- The Montgomery Bus Boycott lasted over a year—not out of convenience, but conviction.
- The Watts uprising, the Stonewall riots, and the March on Washington didn't come from calm—they came from exhaustion.
- Ferguson. Minneapolis. Standing Rock. Atlanta.

These were not breakdowns of order.

They were testimonies.

Moments when people said:

"If this is order, we don't want it.

If this is peace, it ain't ours."

Uprising Is Not Just Reaction—It's Strategy

They will try to frame every protest as impulsive.

They will say the people are acting out of emotion.

But let us be clear:

- A general strike is strategy.
- A rent boycott is strategy.
- A school walkout is strategy.
- Reclaiming land, occupying state buildings, disrupting commerce—this is not rage without reason.

Movements like these are built on:

- WhatsApp chains between tenants
- Secret meetings between workers
- Mutual aid maps, legal defense teams, and community watch networks
- Organizers who sleep in cars, nurses who walk out in protest, teachers who refuse to comply

None of it is random.

It is resistance refined.

It is how the people say:

"This system may not bend,

so we'll break away from it—and build something that won't need bending."

We've Already Changed More Than They Expected

They won't admit it,

but our refusal has already shifted what they thought was fixed.

- The Amazon Labor Union made billionaires flinch.
- Tenants across cities have frozen rent hikes through organizing.
- Students at universities have shut down partnerships with police and demanded divestment from war machines.
- After 2020, millions of people who never joined protests before now know what abolition means.
- Mutual aid networks are feeding, housing, and caring for people faster than the government ever has.

Change doesn't always look like a vote.

Sometimes it looks like people deciding they deserve better—and moving as if it's already true.

The People Are Not Waiting Anymore

We are done with:

- Petitions that gather dust
- Panels that change nothing
- Leaders who ask us to calm down
- Reform that makes us beg for rights we should have been born with

We've lost too much to play polite.

We've buried too many names.

We've watched too many turn into hashtags and documentaries.

while the system reboots and carries on.

Now we carry each other.

Through mutual aid, through protests, through collective grief and radical joy.

Through food drives and bail funds and healing circles and fire.

Across generations—

elders who've marched before,

youth who refuse to march in circles,

and everyone in between—

we rise not as individuals, but as a people who know:

This system won't save us.

But we can save each other.

We don't need to be told what we are allowed to do.

We already know what must be done.

Because What's Coming Is Not Collapse—It's Clarity

There is no going back.

Not after the curtain has been pulled,

not after the mask has slipped.

The people have seen too much.

We feel it in our bodies,

in our schools,

in our jobs,

in our breath.

And now, we move.

We are not afraid of boiling.

We are afraid of waiting so long that the flame goes out.

And we refuse to let that happen.

"In the Middle of the Fireline"

We hear it first—

boots on asphalt, radios crackling,

the hum of breath between chants,

the slow rhythm of hope pressed

against the pace of fear.

We see each other—

bandanas pulled tight, signs held high,

eyes sharp with memory,

banners stitched from kitchen rags

and funeral shirts.

We smell smoke—

not just from tear gas,

but from the fried chicken somebody brought

to feed the line

and the sage lit by the healer

circling our shoulders like a prayer.

We taste dust,

rubber,

salt from tears not born of sorrow

but strategy—

because we've been planning,

organizing,

pulling late nights printing flyers

and prepping jail funds

and passing encrypted links

so they can't find our maps.

We feel the heat of each other's backs,

elbow to elbow—

artists beside lawyers beside grandmas beside hackers

beside the kid who came alone

but never stood alone again.

We touch the ground—

not just with our bodies

but with our purpose.

We don't run.

We hold.

Even when they circle with shields,

even when they lie on camera,

even when the news spins silence

and the drones blink above us

like fake stars watching a story

they'll never understand.

We've read the books,

trained the medics,

seeded the gardens,

written the policies

we'll live by when this crumbles.

We don't just protest.

We prepare.

We don't just resist.

We build.

We smell the smoke—

but we also smell rain.

We see the enemy—

but we see the future, too,

leaning on crutches,

bandaged, breathing,

but standing.

This is what uprising tastes like:

like sweat,

like ash,

like freedom

coming slow,

but coming still.

PART THREE

RECLAIMING POWER

How we take back a new system on our own terms

From the Fields to the Throne

Black Leaders and Self-Governance

We were never meant to rule.

Not in their world. Not in the system built to keep us in chains, fields, cages, or contracts.

Our leadership was always meant to be silenced, doubted, or used—but never trusted with power.

And yet, we led.

We led when we had no titles.

We led when no one gave us permission.

We led when leadership looked like feeding a hungry block, hiding freedom seekers in basements, or holding your head up while the world tried to bow it down.

Now we're in the moment of return.

Not to the table they built, but to the thrones we've been carving with our own hands.

This is not a plea for inclusion. It is a blueprint for self-governance.

The Lie of Representation Without Power

They told us that representation was the goal.

"Put a Black face in a white space," they said,

"and you've won something."

But what is the use of a crown made of glass ceilings?

What is the value of a seat at a table that still serves poisoned plates?

We've watched too many of our own step into "power,"

only to find the tools they were handed

were built to maintain the very system we were trying to dismantle.

We've seen:

- Black mayors overseeing police budgets that ballooned
- Black prosecutors defending the carceral state
- Black leaders used as shields for policies that still harm Black people

This is not to shame those who rise within.

But it is to ask: What are we rising into?

And what would it mean to rise outside their walls?

We've Governed Ourselves Before

Our legacy of self-governance is long—and powerful.

- During slavery, we created spiritual and mutual aid communities in hush harbors and praise houses—governed by elders, mothers, and chosen leaders.
- In the 19th and early 20th centuries, we built independent Black towns:
    - Rosewood, Florida
    - Greenwood (Tulsa), Oklahoma
    - Seneca Village, a thriving Black land-owning community in New York, razed to build Central Park

    These towns had Black-owned businesses, schools, newspapers, and elected officials.

- In 1898, Wilmington, North Carolina, had a majority-Black leadership in government—until white supremacists launched a violent coup, burning it all to the ground.

But each time we governed ourselves, the state came with fire and gunpowder.

They didn't fear our violence. They feared our vision.

And still, we built.

Modern Movements Rooted in Self-Determination

That legacy lives on.

- Cooperation Jackson in Mississippi is building a community-controlled economy rooted in solidarity, land reclamation, and democratic governance.
- Moms 4 Housing in Oakland reclaimed vacant corporate-owned properties to shelter unhoused Black families and sparked a citywide movement.

- Black farmers, after generations of dispossession, are reclaiming land, creating food sovereignty networks, and returning to cooperative agriculture.
- The Electoral Justice Project—launched by the Movement for Black Lives—supports grassroots political campaigns that build power from the bottom up.
- In cities across the country, activists and educators are building freedom schools, community bail funds, healing collectives, and mutual aid networks that function as forms of local governance beyond the state.

This is self-governance.

Not permission. Not tokenism.

Power in practice.

What Leadership Looks Like Now

It looks like the mother who turns her home into a food pantry.

The artist who turns her work into curriculum.

The teen who runs point on security at a protest because he knows the terrain.

The pastor who offers more than sermons—who opens his church to shelter and strategy.

It's also the organizers running city budgets through people's assemblies,

the lawyers drafting abolitionist policy,

the caregivers turning living rooms into healing spaces,

the grandmothers who remember how to survive without the state.

This is leadership that flows up from the ground, not down from a podium.

Leadership that takes collective care as its first commandment.

Leadership that knows power isn't possession—it's responsibility.

We are not waiting for institutions to accept us.

We are building institutions rooted in us.

The Throne Is Not the Goal—The People Are

We're not trying to become our oppressors.

We are trying to become ungovernable by them.

That means:

- Not waiting for the system to open doors.
- Not craving their titles, their approval, or their applause.
- Knowing that freedom can't be franchised.

We've already started:

One garden. One co-op. One clinic. One block. One curriculum. One liberated space at a time.

We don't just want better leaders.

We want better systems—led by us, for us.

So yes—call us leaders.

But know that our thrones don't sit above the people.

They sit among them.

Because what we are reclaiming

is not just power.

It is purpose.

And that can never be stolen again.

"I Don't Wear the Crown, But I Carry the Weight"

I never liked the spotlight.

Never chased a title,

never needed my name in the bulletin.

But I've been here.

In this neighborhood.

On this block.

For a long, long time.

They talk about leaders on the news,

but I see mine at the laundromat,

in the garden,

under the streetlights

walking someone's baby home from school.

I've done what I was given to do.

Not out of duty,

but because the Lord put something in my hands

and told me,

"Use it."

So I taught when I had no classroom.

Fed folks with food I didn't have extra of.

Listened when nobody else could.

Held people's grief in my chest like communion.

I move quiet.

But I've been there—

at city hall meetings they hoped we wouldn't attend.

In church basements,

planning tomorrow while the world slept.

At hospital bedsides,

watching strong women whisper their last breath

and still call it love.

I've seen young ones rise.

Watched them build what we only dreamed of.

They speak louder.

They move faster.

And I thank God for it.

Because they're not just fighting—they're planting.

And I've planted too.

My seeds don't always bloom where folks can see them,

but they grow deep.

They hold things up.

Leadership don't always preach.

Sometimes it just shows up.

Brings water.

Stays late.

Cleans up after the noise is gone.

I don't wear the crown.

But I carry the weight.

And I carry it

with faith,

with quiet hands,

and a heart that never needed to be seen

to know it was sent.

Water from the People
Economic Freedom and Wealth Distribution

They taught us to believe money was power.

But they never told us how power was stolen first—how it was our backs that built this country, our labor that seeded its wealth, our exclusion that protected its hoarded fortunes.

They taught us to dream of riches,

but never told us the truth about the river we were always meant to drink from.

And now—we're remembering.

Because the problem isn't just that we're broke.

The problem is that we were robbed.

And they're still stealing.

Wealth in America Was Built by Extraction

This country's economy has always run on a single engine: take what's not yours.

- Enslaved labor built Southern cotton empires, Wall Street banks, and Ivy League institutions.
- Black farmers lost over 90% of their land in the 20th century—through fraud, violence, and state-backed dispossession.
- Redlining, urban renewal, and predatory lending blocked Black families from homeownership, the primary pathway to generational wealth.
- Indigenous land theft, Chinese exclusion, Mexican labor exploitation, and Black labor underpaid and criminalized—all written into law, all woven into profit.

Globally, the same theft continues under a new name.

- African nations rich in oil, gold, and cobalt have been mined dry by foreign powers.
- Caribbean and Latin American nations are still drowning in IMF and World Bank debt traps, created to keep them dependent.
- Water is privatized in villages where people once drank freely from rivers.
- Crops are exported while locals starve.
- Colonization never ended. It just learned to wear a tie.

So when they say capitalism rewards hard work,

we ask: Whose hands did the work?

And who got paid?

Capitalism Thrives on Hoarding—But We Thrive on Flow

In their system, wealth is treated like a vault.

Locked. Gated. Inherited. Protected.

But in ours?

Wealth was meant to move.

Wealth, like water, only nourishes when it flows.

When it:

- Circulates through hands that need it
- Pours into schools, homes, healthcare, art
- Pools in the places that were once called "blighted" but were actually just starved

Fannie Lou Hamer knew this.

When she started the Freedom Farm Cooperative in 1969, she said,

"If you give a man a piece of land and the seed to plant, and he gets a little help, he can make it."

It wasn't about charity—it was about sovereignty.

Land. Food. Dignity. Shared harvest.

Dr. Claud Anderson warned that no civil rights victory would hold without economic power.

He called for building an economic foundation first—one that keeps dollars circulating within our own communities before being extracted out.

Wealth is not just what you have.

It's what you keep, what you share, and what you grow.

We're Not Waiting for Trickle-Down. We're Digging Canals

If wealth won't move freely, we move it ourselves.

We:

- Start co-ops so labor is owned, not leased
- Organize rent strikes to stop predatory landlords
- Fund neighbors' surgeries, tuition, groceries—no middleman
- Invest in each other's businesses instead of waiting for loans
- Build financial literacy programs our schools won't
- Call out nonprofits that raise millions and give back pennies
- Redirect giving toward grassroots groups that actually serve the people

Our people are designing economies with healing in mind.

Where bartering is honored.

Where community gardens feed families before profits feed investors.

Where Black women fund each other's dreams through lending circles.

Where the payday loan store gets replaced by a community credit union.

Where reparations are not an ask, but a commitment—local, national, global.

We are not rebuilding within capitalism.

We are growing around it.

Wealth Must Be Measured in Health, Not Just Holdings

Wealth isn't just what you can spend.

It's what you can survive.

True wealth is:
- Not being afraid to miss work
- Knowing your kids can see a doctor
- Having time to rest, reflect, and dream bigger than survival
- Being free to fail and still have a safety net
- Passing down more than struggle

Until everyone can do that,

we are still in poverty—no matter how many Black millionaires we parade on magazine covers.

Wealth should not trickle.

It should rush, like water breaking through a dam.

And the dam was never broken by those at the top.

It cracked because the people struck it over and over—together.

The River Is Ours to Redirect

We've been told to beg for what we built.

But we're done begging.

Because we remember:

Our ancestors farmed with no land.

Built with no blueprints.

Saved with no banks.

They taught us that money is not freedom—movement is.

So we build:

Circles, networks, collectives, credit unions, liberation budgets, economic mutuality.

We look to each other, not institutions.

We look inward, not upward.

In Jackson, Mississippi, a single community-run organization began to buy back land block by block.

What started as resistance to gentrification became a blueprint:

- Cooperative housing
- Worker-owned businesses
- Community-run schools
- No police presence—but safety from within

They didn't just survive the system.

They planted something that outgrew it.

This Time, the River Flows From Us

We are no longer waiting for access.

We are designing a new flow.

Because wealth—real wealth—shouldn't be locked in vaults.

It should be passed hand to hand

like water,

like breath,

like freedom.

"The Vault Didn't Save Me"

I once told a woman she was denied.

Application stamped, desk cleared by lunch.

She had three kids,

a late light bill,

a prayer on her lips.

I never looked up.

Just checked the box,

closed the case.

Now I see her face

every time I wake

under a freeway overpass

that smells like burnt plastic

and last night's mistakes.

I was a banker.

Pressed shirts, polished lies.

I knew how to smile and say "unfortunately"

like it meant something.

I knew how to call eviction "policy."

I knew how to sell debt

like it was salvation.

Then the market cracked,

and I fell through.

Fast.

The kind of fall that takes your pride

before it takes your name.

No more house.

No more suit.
No more door code.

And no one—
no one I worked with—
asked where I went.

You know who found me?

A man I denied for a small business loan
five years back.
He remembered my name.
I remembered his jaw tightening
when I said he "didn't qualify."

He handed me a sandwich
wrapped in wax paper
and didn't say a word.
Just nodded
and walked away.

That broke something in me.
Not shame.
Clarity.

Because he still had his dignity.
And I had nothing but stories
of how I helped steal from people
who carried more hope than I ever did.

Now I sit on a crate
outside a bank I once ran,
watching kids carry groceries
for elders with bad knees,

watching neighbors cook on hotplates

for strangers they just met.

There's more wealth on this block

than there ever was behind my desk.

I see money moving

without middlemen.

I see healing

without insurance.

I see power

without title.

They taught me to worship vaults.

But vaults don't feed you.

Vaults don't hold you

when you got nowhere left to be.

What saved me

wasn't a policy.

It was a sandwich.

A nod.

A neighbor.

A moment of undeserved grace

that said:

"You were wrong.

But you're still ours, if you're ready to come back."

Now I give what little I get.

Fix busted carts.

Sweep curbs.

Carry bags.

Because movement

is worth more than money.

And this street

feels more like a kingdom

than my office ever did.

Building Beyond the System

Reclaiming Land, Education, and Community

We were never meant to belong here.

Not to the stolen land, the broken schools, or the cities carved by red lines.

Not to the housing blocks named after generals who signed our displacement.

Not to textbooks that erase us while demanding we pledge allegiance.

We were meant to exist in pieces—

scattered, surveilled, dependent.

Never rooted.

Never whole.

Never home.

And yet—

we are building.

Not to be included.

To be sovereign.

Land Is Not Just Property—It's Possibility

Before it was fenced, paved, or bought,

land was freedom.

It held memory and future, seeds and safety,

ritual and rest.

For Black and Indigenous people especially,

land is not just a resource.

It is a birthright.

A place to become whole again.

Which is why the state feared it.

And stole it.

- Acres promised to freedmen were ripped away within a generation

- Black towns were drowned by floods—or fire
- Indigenous nations were "relocated," then relocated again
- Redlined zones turned into ghettos by design, not chance
- Gentrification dressed up dispossession in lattes and zoning laws

But land is not gone.

We are taking it back.

Through:

- Community land trusts like those in Atlanta, Chicago, and Boston, which keep housing affordable and permanently in the hands of residents—not developers.
- Black farming cooperatives like the Detroit Black Community Food Security Network, which restores both food and sovereignty in urban soil.
- The Land Back movement, where Indigenous nations have reclaimed sacred sites—like the return of the sacred Pe' Sla lands in South Dakota to the Lakota.
- Moms 4 Housing in Oakland, who broke into a vacant home owned by a real estate investment firm and sparked a citywide conversation about who deserves to live—and lead—in their neighborhoods.

We are not renting freedom.

We are planting it.

Education Was Never Neutral—So We're Teaching Ourselves

The school bell has always rung like a siren.

For generations, we were:

- Taught false histories
- Tracked into failure
- Punished for speaking our own truths
- Forced to memorize myths, pledges, and lies

And still, we learned.

In church basements, on porches, in freedom schools, in silence.

Now, we build:

- Liberation curriculums, like those taught at Freedom Home Academy International in Chicago or the Zapatista schools of Chiapas—where education means land, language, and resistance
- Homeschool pods, led by Black parents, that center heritage, truth, and emotional well-being
- Afrocentric schools like the Uhuru Academy and Kamali Academy, which ground students in their culture while teaching critical thinking, business, and self-governance
- Youth-led media collectives producing zines, podcasts, and short films that interrogate the world instead of submitting to it

Because we are done preparing our children for systems that were never built for them.

Now, we prepare them to build their own.

Community Is the New Country

When the state won't protect us,

we protect each other.

When the system won't nourish us,

we feed each other.

When the city turns its back,

we turn to each other.

That's not charity.

That's infrastructure.

Our block captains are better than mayors.

Our neighborhood aunties are better than therapists.

Our art speaks clearer than the news.

Our grief circles heal deeper than courts ever could.

We are building beyond what they gave us.

We are:

- Creating healing centers in barbershops
- Running clinics in churches
- Holding trauma trainings in community kitchens
- Mapping safety with our own hands—no sirens required

This is not a return to anything.

This is a departure.

We Are Not Waiting to Be Free—We Are Living Free Now

They keep asking if revolution is possible.

But they're asking the wrong question.

We're not waiting to start.

We're already here.

Every home reclaimed.

Every child protected.

Every seed planted.

Every lie replaced by truth—

is a border crossed

into a new world.

One where:

- We belong to the land—not to deeds
- We belong to each other—not to prisons
- We belong to truth—not to textbooks
- We belong to ourselves

And that—

that is how nations begin.

And If You Look Close Enough, You'll See It Already Happening

On a quiet street in a forgotten part of the city,

a school is blooming.

Not the kind with metal detectors and silent rows—

but one where elders sit in circles,

teaching children how to grow food,

how to question power,

how to speak their history like a second language.

Next door, a garden's been planted

in a lot that once held nothing but trash and bitterness.

Now, herbs grow wild. Tomatoes climb the fence like laughter.

No one locks the gate.

There's a clinic down the street—

not state-funded, but soul-funded.

Run by a nurse who lost her hospital job for telling the truth,

and now treats neighbors for free.

No paperwork. No judgment. Just healing.

And at night,

the people gather.

They don't sing national anthems.

They read poetry.

They write policies.

They cook for one another.

They plan, dream, fight, rest.

You won't see this on the news.

But this—right here—

is the new country.

It's not built in marble.

It's built in memory, motion, and mercy.

And it belongs to us.

"I Am the Land, and I Remember"

(An Anthem from the Ground Up)

I am the land,
and I remember.

The names you no longer say—
I whispered them when no one else would.
The hands that bled in my soil—
I held them gently.
The feet that fled, the bodies buried,
the crops burned, the children stolen—
I never forgot.

I am the land,
and I remember.

I remember your songs before they were silenced.
Your dances before they were punished.
Your languages before they were banned.
Your gardens before they were paved.
Your homes before they were sold out from under you.

I was not the one who betrayed you.
They built fences.
I held roots.
They built cities.
I held bones.
They poisoned my rivers.
Still, I made them flow.

And now—

you are coming back to me.

With shovels, with seeds,
with stories and sweat.
Not to ask permission.
But to remember
that I was always yours.

You are not trespassers here.
You are not renters of your birthright.
You are not statistics or shadows.
You are the builders.
The growers.
The ones who know that power does not rise from thrones—
it rises from below.

Plant your flags in food and freedom.
Plant your dreams where the concrete cracked.
Let the classroom be the garden,
let the anthem be the drum,
let the blueprint be the people.

I do not belong to their deeds.
I do not answer to their titles.
I rise beneath your bare feet.
I rise when you gather,
when you feed,
when you teach,
when you heal.

I rise when you stop waiting.
And start building.

So sing me,

not in the language of nations,

but in the language of care.

March not for me,

but with me.

Stand not over me,

but in me.

I am the land.

And I remember.

And now—

so do you.

Epilogue: We Remember, We Build

If you've made it here,

then something in you has been waiting—

to speak,

to know,

to remember.

This was never just a book.

It was a gathering.

A homecoming.

A fire lit in the corners where silence used to sit.

Because this system did not lose its way.

It was built this way.

The pain was not accidental.

The poverty was not collateral.

The confusion was not coincidental.

It was engineered.

But so was our survival.

And in these pages, we've named it.

We've told the truth about power—

how it hoards, manipulates, and erases.

We've told the truth about wealth—

how it was extracted, not earned.

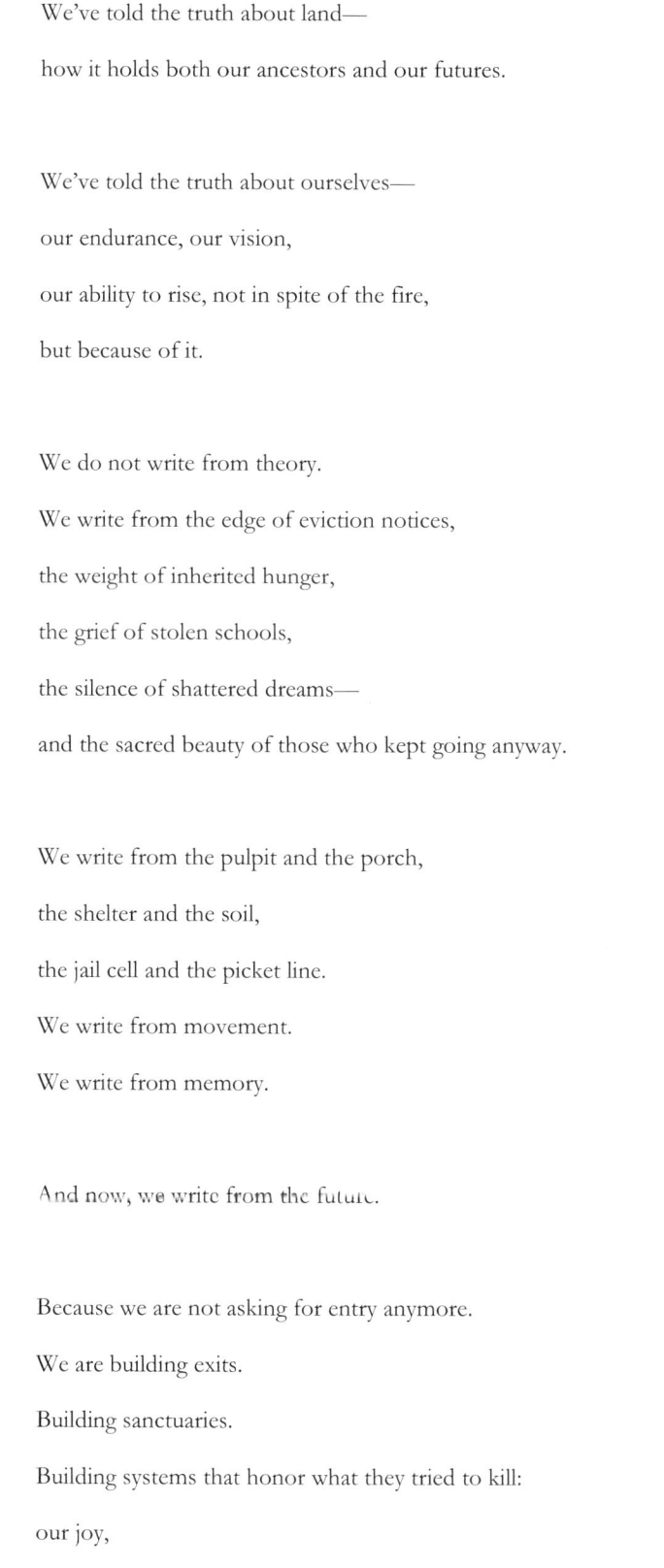

We've told the truth about land—

how it holds both our ancestors and our futures.

We've told the truth about ourselves—

our endurance, our vision,

our ability to rise, not in spite of the fire,

but because of it.

We do not write from theory.

We write from the edge of eviction notices,

the weight of inherited hunger,

the grief of stolen schools,

the silence of shattered dreams—

and the sacred beauty of those who kept going anyway.

We write from the pulpit and the porch,

the shelter and the soil,

the jail cell and the picket line.

We write from movement.

We write from memory.

And now, we write from the future.

Because we are not asking for entry anymore.

We are building exits.

Building sanctuaries.

Building systems that honor what they tried to kill:

our joy,

our genius,

our right to breathe without permission.

We are not free yet.

But we are no longer lost.

We remember where we came from.

We know what was stolen.

And we know what is still ours to build.

So take this book and let it do what it was made to do:

Let it echo in your conversations.

Let it rumble in your spirit when you walk past injustice.

Let it rise in you when you're asked to settle for less.

Let it call you back to the people.

To the root.

To the work.

Because the revolution is not a moment.

It's a rhythm.

It's a restoration.

And it begins again

every time someone like you

refuses to forget.

Final Gesture

To every single person who made it through these pages—thank you.

This wasn't easy to write, and it wasn't meant to be easy to read.

But if it made you feel less alone, more seen, more called to act—then we've already won something.

I wrote this because I needed to remember, too.

References & Acknowledgments

This anthology was crafted not only through lived experiences but also through deep dialogue with influential historical events, movements, intellectual works, and contemporary news sources that shaped the ideas within these pages.

Historical Events

- Clarence Thomas Supreme Court Confirmation Hearings (1991) – Anita Hill's testimony on workplace sexual harassment.
- COINTELPRO (1956–1971) – FBI's targeted suppression of civil rights movements.
- MOVE Bombing, Philadelphia (1985) – Police bombing of the MOVE organization.
- Redlining and Urban Renewal (1930s–Present) – Systematic disenfranchisement of minority communities.
- War on Drugs & Mass Incarceration (1970s–Present) – Legislative structures perpetuating racial disparities in incarceration.

Intellectual Influences

- Alexander, Michelle. The New Jim Crow. New Press, 2010.
- Baldwin, James. Collected essays.
- Davis, Angela Y. Are Prisons Obsolete? Seven Stories Press, 2003.
- Du Bois, W.E.B. Black Reconstruction in America. Harcourt, Brace, 1935.
- Fanon, Frantz. The Wretched of the Earth. Grove Press, 1963.
- Gilmore, Ruth Wilson. Golden Gulag. University of California Press, 2007.
- hooks, bell. Teaching to Transgress. Routledge, 1994.
- Lorde, Audre. "The Master's Tools Will Never Dismantle the Master's House," Sister Outsider. Crossing Press, 1984.
- Malcolm X. Selected speeches and writings.

Movements & Community Organizations

- Black Lives Matter – Addressing systemic racism and police brutality.
- Cooperation Jackson – Economic democracy initiatives in Jackson, MS.
- Detroit Black Community Food Security Network – Food sovereignty and land reclamation efforts.
- Freedom Schools – Civil rights education initiatives.
- Highlander Research & Education Center – Training center for grassroots movements.
- Land Back Movement – Indigenous-led land reclamation.
- Moms 4 Housing – Advocating housing as a human right.
- Mutual Aid Networks – Grassroots community support initiatives.
- Uhuru Academy, Kamali Academy – Afrocentric education models.
- Zapatista Autonomous Education – Indigenous education resistance in Chiapas, Mexico.

Media & News Sources (Headlines Cited in Poems)

- "Breonna Taylor Was Shot and Killed by Louisville Police During a Botched Raid." The New York Times, March 13, 2020.
- "Elijah McClain's Death Raises Calls for Justice After Police Encounter." The Guardian, June 25, 2020.
- "Flint Water Crisis: Everything You Need to Know." CNN, April 25, 2016.
- "George Floyd's Death Sparks Nationwide Protests Against Police Brutality." Washington Post, May 26, 2020.
- "Homeless Moms Take Over Vacant Oakland Home to Protest Housing Crisis." NBC News, December 4, 2019.
- "Land Back: Indigenous-Led Movements Push for Return of Ancestral Lands." Indian Country Today, August 16, 2020.
- "MOVE Bombing: Remembering the Day Philadelphia Bombed Its Own Citizens." TIME Magazine, May 13, 2020.
- "Puerto Rico's Complicated History with the FBI and the Fight for Independence." NPR, May 5, 2021.
- "Redlining's Legacy: Maps That Shaped Our Cities." National Geographic, October 17, 2016.
- "The 1994 Crime Bill and Its Legacy of Mass Incarceration." The Atlantic, September 13, 2019.

Personal & Collective Gratitude

Special acknowledgment is extended to all activists, thinkers, teachers, everyday builders, ancestors, and future generations who carry this work forward—thank you.

We Remember, We Build

A Final Word from T. E. Door

I did not come to this world to survive in silence.
I came to name what tried to break us.
To pull truth from the smoke.
To build with words what this world has buried.

I do this for the mothers with calloused hands and breaking hearts.
For the children who've learned to pray for peace before they've learned to spell.
For the ones who carry brilliance but are always told they're too loud, too angry, too much.
For my babies—who deserve a world that does not require suffering for strength.

This book is not a mirror. It is a lantern.
A reminder that our stories are not too heavy to hold.
That our rage can be righteous. That our hope can be sharpened.
That your voice, your grief, your memory—it matters.

If you've made it this far, I thank you.
Not just for reading, but for staying with me in this flame.
You are the reason we remember.
You are the reason we build.
And you are proof that nothing planted in love will ever go to waste.

So, carry this with you.
Let it stir something.
And when the world grows cold again—
remember: you are the heat they cannot put out.

— T.E. Door

Made in the USA
Columbia, SC
09 July 2025

90ff9645-2d9c-4487-b44b-a2ef0cad8fbaR02